Mary

Seeing God through the Eyes of a Mother

Drawn in
BIBLE STUDY

Eugene H. Peterson

THE**MESSAGE**

NAVPRESS

*A NavPress resource published in alliance
with Tyndale House Publishers, Inc.*

NAVPRESS⬤®

NavPress is the publishing ministry of The Navigators, an international Christian organization and leader in personal spiritual development. NavPress is committed to helping people grow spiritually and enjoy lives of meaning and hope through personal and group resources that are biblically rooted, culturally relevant, and highly practical.

For more information, visit www.NavPress.com.

Mary: Seeing God through the Eyes of a Mother

Copyright © 2017 by Eugene H. Peterson. All rights reserved.

A NavPress resource published in alliance with Tyndale House Publishers, Inc.

NAVPRESS, the NAVPRESS logo, *THE MESSAGE*, and THE MESSAGE logo are registered trademarks of NavPress, The Navigators, Colorado Springs, CO. *TYNDALE* is a registered trademark of Tyndale House Publishers, Inc. Absence of ® in connection with marks of NavPress or other parties does not indicate an absence of registration of those marks.

The Team:
Don Pape, Publisher
David Zimmerman, Editor
Jennifer Ghionzoli, Designer

Cover and interior illustrations are the property of their respective copyright holders, and all rights are reserved. Cover illustration by Lizzie Preston © NavPress; cover watercolor texture © Charles Perrault/Adobe Stock. Interior borders and other images on pages 4, 14, and 15 © Felicity French/Advocate Inc.; interior geometric pattern © Vítek Prchal/Creative Market; all other interior illustrations by Lizzie Preston, Angelika Scudamore, and Jennifer Tucker © NavPress.

The author is represented by the literary agency of Alive Literary Agency, 7680 Goddard St., Suite 200, Colorado Springs, CO 80920, www.aliveliterary.com.

All Scripture quotations are taken from *THE MESSAGE*, copyright © 1993, 1994, 1995, 1996, 2000, 2001, 2002 by Eugene H. Peterson. Used by permission of NavPress. All rights reserved. Represented by Tyndale House Publishers, Inc.

Some content from the introduction and "How to Get the Most out of Mary" is adapted from *Eat This Book*, copyright © 2006 by Eugene H. Peterson. Published by Eerdmans. Reprinted by permission of the publisher; all rights reserved. Some content is adapted from *Five Smooth Stones for Pastoral Work*, copyright © 1992 by Eugene H. Peterson. Published by Eerdmans. Reprinted by permission of the publisher; all rights reserved. Some content is adapted from Eugene H. Peterson, *Living the Resurrection* (Colorado Springs: NavPress, 2006). Some content from "How to Lead a Drawn In Bible Study" is adapted from Eugene H. Peterson, *The Wisdom of Each Other* (Grand Rapids, MI: Zondervan, 1998). The quotation from Tricia McCary Rhodes is from "Bible Study Meets Crafting," *Her.meneutics*, July 5, 2016, accessed July 8, 2016, at www.christianitytoday.com/women/2016/july/bible-study-meets -crafting-bible-journaling-craze.html?paging=off.

For information about special discounts for bulk purchases, please contact Tyndale House Publishers at csresponse@tyndale.com or call 800-323-9400.

ISBN 978-1-63146-785-1

Printed in China

23	22	21	20	19	18	17
7	6	5	4	3	2	1

contents

introduction

Eugene H. Peterson

READING IS THE FIRST THING, just reading the Bible. As we read, we enter a new world of words and find ourselves in on a conversation in which God has the first and last words. God uses words to form and bless us, to teach and guide us, to forgive and save us.

I didn't start out as a pastor. I began my vocational life as a teacher and for several years taught the biblical languages of Hebrew and Greek in a theological seminary. I expected to live the rest of my life as a professor and scholar, teaching and writing and studying. But then my life took a sudden vocational turn to pastoring a congregation.

I was now plunged into quite a different world. The first noticeable difference was that nobody seemed to care much about the Bible, which so recently people had been paying me to teach them. Many of the people I now worked with knew virtually nothing about it, had never read it, and weren't interested in learning. Many others had spent years reading it, but for them it had gone flat through familiarity, reduced to clichés. Bored, they dropped it. And there weren't many people in between. Very few were interested in what I considered my primary work: getting the words of the Bible into their heads and hearts, getting the message lived. They found newspapers and magazines, videos and pulp fiction more to their taste.

Meanwhile I had taken on as my life work the responsibility for getting these very people to listen—really listen—to the message in this book. I knew I had my work cut out for me.

I lived in two language worlds, the world of the Bible and the world of today. I had always assumed they were the same world. But these people didn't see it that way. So out of necessity I became a "translator" (although I wouldn't have called it that then), daily standing on the border between two worlds, getting the language of the Bible that God uses to create and save us, heal and bless us, judge and rule over us, into the language of today that we use to gossip and tell stories, give directions and do business, sing songs and talk to our children.

My intent is simply to get people reading the Bible who don't know that the Bible is readable at all, at least by them, and to get people who long ago lost interest in the Bible to read it again. Read in order to live, praying as you read, "God, let it be with me just as you say."

INTRODUCTION TO MARY

Scattered throughout the accounts of the life of Jesus known as the Gospels are occasional, brief glimpses of Mary, Jesus' mother. So brief are these passages that we may wonder at the attention and reverence shown to Mary throughout Christian history. How could so few words about her engender so much veneration?

Except, of course, that she's the mother of Jesus. As his mother, she had a unique contribution, a unique vantage point, in his earthly life and ministry. She is the woman who raised Jesus in the way of the people of God, the woman who took him to the Temple for a blessing, the woman who chastised him for lingering at the Temple when he should have been keeping up with the family. Jesus would have watched Mary practice the Jewish rituals that recalled God's saving action in Egypt, God's provision in the harvest, God's abiding presence in creation. To the extent that Jesus *learned* God in his childhood, he *learned* a great deal about him from Mary.

Jesus' mother was a woman in a time when women were undervalued. Not by God, however. Throughout Scripture, God gave women a place of value. The first named people we meet in the story of the Exodus—God's deliverance of the Jews from Egypt, which established so much of Jewish faith and practice—are Shiphrah and Puah, two Hebrew midwives from the lowest social and economic strata of that society (Exodus 1:15-16). These two women set in motion the chain of events that would result in the salvation of the Hebrew people.

World leaders are minor players in the biblical way of writing and participating in history. In contrast, people like Shiphrah and Puah—and, as we'll see, Mary the mother of Jesus—play decisive roles in God's story. Only when we understand this and embrace it will we be in a position to participate wholeheartedly in the work of God's salvation.

Nevertheless, salvation is *God's* work, not ours. Our sight is limited, our steps tentative. That is how we best traverse the landscape of faith—humbly rather than capably.

That humility is exemplified by Mary in her prayer accepting the vocation of mother of God; it is perhaps also exemplified by her willingness to fade into the background of Jesus' story, to participate in God's salvation without losing sight of the fact that this salvation is God's work—for her, and for all of us.

Read in order to live,
PRAYING
as you read,
"God, let it be with me
just as you say."
Eugene Peterson

HOW TO GET THE MOST OUT OF

Mary

*It takes more than bread
to stay alive. It takes a steady
stream of words from God's mouth.*

MATTHEW 4:4

MANY PEOPLE APPROACH READING the Bible as a religious duty or a way to get in good with God. Worse still, some believe God will send a horrible punishment if they don't dedicate at least a half hour each day to dutiful study of his Word. Coming to the Bible with so much religious baggage takes all the fun out of reading it.

Reading the Bible isn't simply a fact-finding mission. You don't come just to collect bits of trivia about God. From the moment you read the first line of the Bible, you will discover that this book isn't about you. It's about God. God gave his Word as the place where you meet him face-to-face.

In order to read the Scriptures adequately and

accurately, it's necessary at the same time to live them—to live them *as* we read them. This kind of reading has been named by our ancestors as *lectio divina*, often translated "spiritual reading." It means not only reading the text but also meditating on the text, praying the text, and living the text. It is reading that enters our souls the way food enters our stomachs, spreads through our blood, and transforms us. Christians don't simply learn or study or use Scripture; we feed on it. Words spoken and listened to, written and read are intended to do something in us, to give us health and wholeness, vitality and holiness, wisdom and hope.

The Scriptures not only reveal everything of who God is but also everything of who we are. And this revelation is done in such a way as to invite participation on both sides, of author and reader.

This may be the single most important thing to know as we come to read and study and believe these Holy Scriptures: this rich, alive, personally revealing God as experienced in Father, Son, and Holy Spirit, personally addressing us in whatever circumstances we find ourselves, at whatever age we are, in whatever state we are. Christian reading is participatory reading, receiving the words in such a way that they become interior to our lives, the rhythms and images becoming practices of prayer, acts of obedience, ways of love. We submit our lives to this text so that God's will may be done on earth as it is in heaven.

One of the characteristic marks of the biblical story-tellers is a certain reticence. They don't tell us too much. They leave a lot of blanks in the narration, an implicit invitation to enter the story ourselves, just as we are, and to discover for ourselves how to fit in. There are, of course, always moral, theological, and historical elements in these stories that need to be studied, but never in dismissal of the story that is being told.

When we submit our lives to what we read in Scripture, we find that we're being led not to see God in our stories but to see our stories in God's. God is the larger context and plot in which our stories find themselves.

The Bible is God's Word. He spoke it into existence, and he continues to speak through it as you read. He doesn't just share words on a page. He shares himself. As you meet God in this conversation, you won't just learn *about* him; you will *experience* him more deeply and more personally than you ever thought possible.

DRAWN IN BIBLE STUDIES

We all lead busy lives, and even when we step away from our activities for spiritual rest and renewal, our activities don't necessarily step away from us. *Drawn in* Bible Studies are designed to temporarily relieve you of distractions so you can enjoy the story of God more fully. This happens in a variety of ways:

The Coloring

For people of all ages, coloring offers a structured activity that fosters creative thinking. Tricia McCary Rhodes, author of *The Wired Soul*, is not surprised by the appeal of coloring among adults today:

> Brain scans of people involved in activities like coloring reveal that as we focus, our heart rate slows and our brain waves enter a more relaxed state. Over time, by engaging in Scripture or prayer art-journaling, it may become easier for us to focus and pay attention in other areas of our lives as well. It is no wonder we are so drawn to this activity.

As you work through a study, read the appropriate Bible passage and question, and mull over your response as you color. Some art has been provided for you, but feel free to draw in the open space as well. The act of coloring will help your "orienting response," the brain function that allows you to filter out background distractions and attend to the matter at hand. That's one reason so many people doodle as they read or study. Ironically, by coloring as you engage in this Bible study, you'll be more attentive to what the Scriptures have to teach you.

The Message

For many people, the Bible has become so familiar that it loses some of its resonance. They've memorized so many Scriptures, or heard so many sermons, that they think they've figured a passage out. For others, the Bible has never not been intimidating—its names and contexts separated from us by millennia, its story shrouded by memories of bad church experiences or negative impressions of people who claim it as their authority. While you can read any Bible translation you like alongside the _Drawn in_ Bible Studies, included in the studies themselves are passages from *The Message*, a rendering of the Bible in contemporary language that matches the tone and informality of the original ancient language. You will often be surprised by the way *The Message* translates something you may have read or heard many times before. And in that surprise, you'll be more receptive for what God might have for you today.

The Questions

When we sit down just to read the Bible, we can feel a bit disoriented. The questions in the _Drawn in_ Bible Studies are designed to help you stay connected to your own lived experience even as you enter into the lived experience of the people and places the Scriptures introduce us to. You'll grow in your understanding of the Bible, but you'll also grow in your understanding of yourself. These questions are also good for discussion—get together with a group of friends, and enjoy coloring and talking together.

The Commentary

Included in this *Drawn in* Bible Study are occasional comments from renowned Bible teacher Eugene Peterson. You'll see his name following his comments. He helps clarify more confusing passages and offers insight into what's behind what you're reading. He'll help keep you from getting stuck.

Leader's Notes

In the section "How to Lead a *Drawn in* Bible Study" you'll find general guidelines for leading people through this study, along with notes specific to each session. These can inform and enhance your experience, so even if you are going through this study on your own, or if you are not the leader of a group discussion of this study, read through the notes as preparation for each session. Nevertheless, don't feel pressure to be an expert; the main purpose of this study is to provide an opportunity for fun and fellowship as people encounter God's Word and consider how it touches their lives.

—SESSION ONE—

You're Beautiful with God's Beauty

LUKE 1:26-56

MOST OF US, most of the time, feel left out. We don't belong. "Insiders" know the ropes; they're in a club from which we are excluded. But with God there are no outsiders. Jesus includes those who typically were treated as outsiders: women, common laborers, the radically different, the poor. He will not countenance religion as a club.

—EUGENE

2 · Mary

1. *Reflect on a time when you were left out. How did it feel? Were you angry? Sad? Anxious? Why?*

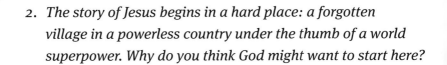

2. *The story of Jesus begins in a hard place: a forgotten village in a powerless country under the thumb of a world superpower. Why do you think God might want to start here?*

———————— ❧ ————————

IN THE SIXTH month of Elizabeth's pregnancy, God sent the angel Gabriel to the Galilean village of Nazareth to a virgin engaged to be married to a man descended from David. His name was Joseph, and the virgin's name, Mary. Upon entering, Gabriel greeted her:

> Good morning!
> You're beautiful with God's beauty,
> Beautiful inside and out!
> God be with you.

She was thoroughly shaken, wondering what was behind a greeting like that. But the angel assured her, "Mary, you have nothing to fear. God has a surprise for you: You will become pregnant and give birth to a son and call his name Jesus.

> He will be great,
>   be called 'Son of the Highest.'
> The Lord God will give him
>   the throne of his father David;
> He will rule Jacob's house forever—
>   no end, ever, to his kingdom."

LUKE 1:26-33 ⎯⎯⎯⎯⎯⎯⎯⎯⎯⎯⎯⎯⎯⎯⎯⎯⎯

3. *You wake up, and an angel is standing in front of you, saying, "Good morning!" What do you do? How do you feel?*

4. *Mary was "thoroughly shaken," but the angel reassures Mary, "You have nothing to fear." What is it about an encounter with God (or, in Mary's case, an angel of God) that can be so overwhelming?*

If you found yourself in such a situation, what do you think would be the proper response to God?

5. *Mary's life prospects are not great, but the angel assures her that this child God is giving her will be a king. Why should she believe him?*

———— ❧ ————

MARY SAID TO the angel, "But how? I've never slept with a man." The angel answered,

The Holy Spirit will come upon you,
    the power of the Highest hover over you;
Therefore, the child you bring to birth
    will be called Holy, Son of God.

"And did you know that your cousin Elizabeth conceived a son, old as she is? Everyone called her barren, and here she is six months pregnant! Nothing, you see, is impossible with God."

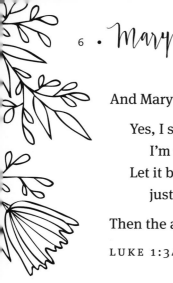

And Mary said,

> Yes, I see it all now:
>> I'm the Lord's maid, ready to serve.
> Let it be with me
>> just as you say.

Then the angel left her.

LUKE 1:34-38 ————————————————

6. *There's the promise, and then there's the path. What is unique about this pregnancy God is promising to Mary?*

When has God taken you down an unexpected path toward something he's crafted for your life?

7. *This pregnancy will clearly be miraculous. How might Mary be reassured by the angel's comments about her cousin Elizabeth?*

8. *"Nothing, you see, is impossible with God." Do you believe that? What makes it hard to believe?*

9. *Mary agrees to the angel's proposition. What does that tell you about her?*

   Do you find it easy or hard to believe God's promises? Why?

10. *How would you respond to the angel's offer? What would make it hard to accept? What would make you want to accept it?*

— ⤶ —

MARY DIDN'T WASTE a minute. She got up and traveled to a town in Judah in the hill country, straight to Zachariah's house, and greeted Elizabeth. When Elizabeth heard Mary's greeting, the baby in her womb leaped. She was filled with the Holy Spirit, and sang out exuberantly,

> You're so blessed among women,
>> and the babe in your womb, also blessed!
> And why am I so blessed that
>> the mother of my Lord visits me?
> The moment the sound of your
>> greeting entered my ears,
> The babe in my womb
>> skipped like a lamb for sheer joy.
> Blessed woman, who believed what God said,
>> believed every word would come true!

LUKE 1:39-45 ————————————————————

11. *Why do you think Mary is in such a hurry to visit Elizabeth?*

12. *What is it about Mary that causes Elizabeth to call her "so blessed among women"?*

_____ ⟋⟍ _____

AND MARY SAID,

I'm bursting with God-news;
I'm dancing the song of my Savior God.
God took one good look at me, and look what
happened—
I'm the most fortunate woman on earth!
What God has done for me will never be forgotten,
the God whose very name is holy, set apart from
all others.
His mercy flows in wave after wave
on those who are in awe before him.
He bared his arm and showed his strength,
scattered the bluffing braggarts.
He knocked tyrants off their high horses,
pulled victims out of the mud.
The starving poor sat down to a banquet;
the callous rich were left out in the cold.
He embraced his chosen child, Israel;
he remembered and piled on the mercies, piled
them high.
It's exactly what he promised,
beginning with Abraham and right up to now.

Mary stayed with Elizabeth for three months and then
went back to her own home.

LUKE 1:46-56 ─────────────────────

"HIS MERCY FLOWS IN WAVE AFTER WAVE ON THOSE WHO ARE in awe before him."

FROM LUKE 1.
THE MESSAGE

13. *A pregnant, unmarried young woman might be considered scandalous in Mary's culture, but here she declares herself "the most fortunate woman on earth." Why does she consider herself so fortunate?*

14. *Mary's song moves quickly from celebrating her pregnancy to celebrating God. What do you find most compelling among all the things she sings about him?*

A NOTE FROM EUGENE

BEFORE MARY PRAYED a half-dozen words, we realize that this girl knew her family story—the Holy Scriptures—which tells the ways that God has been speaking and working among his people. The heart of Mary's prayer involves three great reversals: (1) God establishes his strength and disestablishes the proud; (2) God puts down the people at the top and lifts up the people at the bottom; and (3) God fills the hungry and sends the rich away empty.

"The starving poor

SAT DOWN TO A BANQUET,

the callous rich were

LEFT OUT IN THE COLD."

from Luke 1,

MSG

15. Mary declares that everything she sings about—including her pregnancy—is "exactly what [God] promised, beginning with Abraham and right up to now." What promises do you think she's talking about?

What promises has God made to you?

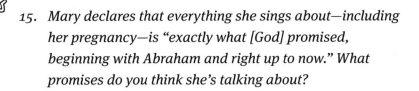

REFLECT *on your own life story. When can you recall that God "piled on the mercies, piled them high"?*

When can you recall that God "showed his strength"?

This passage of Scripture is a celebration of this special calling given to Mary. But Mary will face challenges as well. How does God's presence in your life make facing such challenges easier for you?

Prayer

God, the world you have made for us
    is pregnant with potential.
It's easy to feel small in such a world.
But we are ourselves expanded by your promise.
Enlarge our imaginations, God.
Make us grateful, joyful participants
    in what is yet to come.
Help us to bear your hope, your confidence,
    your blessing for the world around us.

Mary

Whatever He Tells You

JOHN 2:1-12

JESUS IS STILL at work in his creation today. Still performing signs that point to him. Still revealing not only his glory but his goodness. And, most particularly, his goodness toward us.

—EUGENE

1. *Think back on the past week. What has happened that might have been Jesus revealing his goodness to you?*

2. *Have you noticed yourself thinking about God at all this week? If so, what do you think prompted you to think about him?*

If not, what did you find yourself thinking about? How might God relate to what occupied your mind this week?

———————— ✄ ————————

*T*HERE WAS A wedding in the village of Cana in Galilee. Jesus' mother was there. Jesus and his disciples were guests also. When they started running low on wine at the wedding banquet, Jesus' mother told him, "They're just about out of wine."

Jesus said, "Is that any of our business, Mother—yours or mine? This isn't my time. Don't push me."

She went ahead anyway, telling the servants, "Whatever he tells you, do it."

JOHN 2:1-5 ————————————————————

3. *Jesus has disciples by this time—throughout Galilee he will become "the talk of the town" (see Luke 4:36-37). And yet he still is his mother's son, with family obligations like weddings. What does it say about Jesus that he takes time to attend this local wedding?*

4. *Mary points out to Jesus that "they're just about out of wine," but Jesus responds with "Is that any of our business, Mother—yours or mine? . . . Don't push me." Are you surprised by the tone Jesus takes with his mother? Why or why not?*

5. *Jesus has already recruited followers. One even proclaimed Jesus "the Son of God, the King of Israel!" (see John 1:49). Still, here Jesus tells Mary, "This isn't my time." What do you think he means by that?*

IT HAS LONG been customary for readers of John's Gospel to count seven signs, miraculous acts by which we may come to see and believe the revelation of God in Jesus. *Believe* is the critical verb here. The signs are particularly chosen for their power to evoke belief. Changing the water into wine is the first of the seven signs.

6. *Mary ignores Jesus' comments and tells the servants, "Whatever he tells you, do it." What strikes you about the nature of Jesus' relationship with his mother in this passage?*

7. *When have you felt like you had to talk God into doing something? How did that work out?*

What does it say about God that Jesus could be talked into a miracle here?

———— ✿ ————

SIX STONEWARE WATER pots were there, used by the Jews for ritual washings. Each held twenty to thirty gallons. Jesus ordered the servants, "Fill the pots with water." And they filled them to the brim.

"Now fill your pitchers and take them to the host," Jesus said, and they did.

When the host tasted the water that had become wine (he didn't know what had just happened but the servants, of course, knew), he called out to the bridegroom, "Everybody I know begins with their finest wines and after the guests have had their fill brings in the cheap stuff. But you've saved the best till now!"

This act in Cana of Galilee was the first sign Jesus gave, the first glimpse of his glory. And his disciples believed in him.

JOHN 2:6-11 ————————————————

8. Jesus does go ahead and perform a miracle here, and it's a big one: water in six stoneware water pots used for ritual washing, each holding twenty to thirty gallons, turned to wine. That's nearly as much water as every American uses every day. Why would Jesus make such a big gesture after being so reluctant to get involved?

9. Mary and Jesus have both taken risks in this story, but now the servants are taking a risk, bringing what they assume to be water to the host of the wedding. What would you have done? Would you have refused? Asked questions? Done as Jesus asked? Something else? Why?

10. *The host congratulated the bridegroom on the quality of this wine. Why doesn't Jesus get the credit? Why doesn't he (or Mary) ask for the credit?*

11. *"This act . . . was the first sign Jesus gave, the first glimpse of his glory." What does it say about Jesus that creating more than a hundred gallons of fine wine is "the first glimpse of his glory"?*

A NOTE
FROM
EUGENE

SERVANTS GO ABOUT their work quietly and deferentially. There's no person, no matter how weak or useless, to whom they don't stand as servants. To be a servant is to be like God, for God is in his creation serving it, providing everything from food for the sparrow to forgiveness for the sinner. Christ is the best visual aid of what that looks like.

12. This was Jesus' "first glimpse of his glory," but he already had followers, and clearly Mary believed he could make something big happen. How do you explain Mary's early faith in Jesus?

13. What are some experiences that have helped you believe in God's goodness? In God's power?

FTER THIS HE went down to Capernaum along with his mother, brothers, and disciples, and stayed several days.

JOHN 2:12

14. *Jesus' next big act is to create a scene at the Temple in Jerusalem (see John 2:13-25). But for now "he went down to Capernaum along with his mother, brothers, and disciples, and stayed several days." What does it say about Jesus that his major moves are interspersed with these private moments with family and friends?*

15. *Mary's role in this story is pretty modest. But without her prodding, it seems as though Jesus wouldn't have performed this miracle. How does God use our modest actions today to help people to "see and believe the revelation of God in Jesus"?*

    How would you like to see God use you in the next week?

Until we meet again

LOOK AT *your calendar for the next couple of weeks. Where will you be? What will you be doing? Like Mary, be prepared to ask God to act in those places. And when you ask God to act, be prepared as well to encourage people, "Whatever he tells you, do it."*

YOU MAY FIND *yourself in situations like the bridal party in this passage, who ran out of wine at the wedding, or like the servants, who put themselves at risk because Jesus told them to. This passage shows Jesus' goodness, even in secret. This week, ask Jesus to act in situations where you need help. And when you notice that things have gone well for you, thank Jesus for always having your good in mind.*

WHERE *can you fit some private time with God into your calendar over the next couple of weeks?*

Prayer

God, so much of life feels like a minefield,
*   just waiting to explode*
*   in embarrassment, pain, or frustration.*
We feel that for ourselves;
*   we also feel it for our friends, our family,*
*   even strangers who stir us to compassion.*
You are a God of action, so act in these situations.
Spare us and our loved ones the embarrassment,
*   the pain, the frustration—*
*   and we will give you glory for it.*

Mary

Sawing Off the Branch on Which You're Sitting

MARK 3:20-35

COMMON AS BELIEF in God is, there is also an enormous amount of guesswork and gossip surrounding the subject, which results in runaway superstition, anxiety, and exploitation. Mark's Gospel doesn't want us to waste a minute of these precious lives of ours ignorant of this most practical of all matters—that God is passionate to save us.

—EUGENE

1. Who has had the most influence on how you think about God? What made them so influential for you?

How do you think most people arrive at their understanding of God? What do you think is the best way of testing the reliability of people's opinions about God?

2. What have you heard people say about God that might cause someone to experience "anxiety and exploitation"? How have you seen people use God to harm other people?

3. Where do you turn for your information about God? How do you eliminate the guesswork?

A NOTE
FROM
EUGENE **THE CONCERN OF** Mark's Gospel is that we see something significant about the reign of God breaking into our lives—that we would see Jesus as the first ray of light in the dawn of God's Kingdom. That reign is eternally present, which means it is present now, penetrating deeply into us without passing over anything peripheral.

---

*J*ESUS CAME HOME and, as usual, a crowd gathered—so many making demands on him that there wasn't even time to eat. His friends heard what was going on and went to rescue him, by force if necessary. They suspected he was getting carried away with himself.

MARK 3:20-21

They suspected HE WAS GETTING carried away WITH HIMSELF.

FROM MARK 3, MSG

4. *Jesus' friends try to rescue him: "They suspected he was getting carried away with himself." Do you think Jesus' friends are concerned about him or embarrassed by him? Why?*

If you had been with Jesus, what would you have found embarrassing? What would have concerned you about him?

---

*T*HE RELIGION SCHOLARS from Jerusalem came down spreading rumors that he was working black magic, using devil tricks to impress them with spiritual power. Jesus confronted their slander with a story: "Does it make sense to send a devil to catch a devil, to use Satan to get rid of Satan? A constantly squabbling family disintegrates. If Satan were fighting Satan, there soon wouldn't be any Satan left. Do you think it's possible in broad daylight to enter the house of an awake, able-bodied man, and walk off with his possessions unless you tie him up first? Tie him up, though, and you can clean him out.

"Listen to this carefully. I'm warning you. There's nothing done or said that can't be forgiven. But if you persist in your slanders against God's Holy Spirit, you are repudiating the very One who forgives, sawing off the branch on which you're sitting, severing by your own perversity all connection with the One who forgives." He gave this warning because they were accusing him of being in league with Evil.

MARK 3:22-30 ———————————————

5. *Jesus has by this point healed a lot of people, some in very public and spectacular ways. Why do you think he's meeting with such a hostile response?*

6. *Some people go so far as to suggest that Jesus is "in league with Evil." Jesus dismisses that argument as illogical: "Does it make sense . . . to use Satan to get rid of Satan?" What do you think of that argument?*

7. *Have you ever seen someone use "devil tricks" to impress people with "spiritual power"? Why does religion seem so vulnerable to that kind of abuse and exploitation?*

How is Jesus different?

8. *Jesus warns people not to slander the Holy Spirit—*
   "the very One who forgives." What do you think he
   means by that?

9. *What's so bad about being skeptical about someone*
   who claims to be God? Why would Jesus be so stern
   in his warning here?

---

*J*UST THEN HIS mother and brothers showed up. Standing outside, they relayed a message that they wanted a word with him. He was surrounded by the crowd when he was given the message, "Your mother and brothers and sisters are outside looking for you."

Jesus responded, "Who do you think are my mother and brothers?" Looking around, taking in everyone seated around him, he said, "Right here, right in front of you—my mother and my brothers. Obedience is thicker than blood. The person who obeys God's will is my brother and sister and mother."

MARK 3:31-35 ————————————————

10. *Mary now enters the story, along with Jesus' brothers: "They wanted a word with him." What would you guess they want to say?*

11. *Jesus gets the message but addresses the crowd: "Who do you think are my mother and brothers?" Why do you think he'd say this now?*

12. *How do you think Mary would have reacted to Jesus' statement here? How would you have reacted?*

A NOTE
FROM
EUGENE

A CONVERSATION WITH God isn't regulated by social or class distinctions. All men, women, and children, widows and judges, kings and beggars, the literate and the illiterate, poor and rich, the wise and fools, saints and sinners are peers with equal access to God.

13. We're not told that Jesus doesn't meet with Mary and his brothers; we're just given this comment he makes to the crowd. What lesson do you think the crowd took away from Jesus' comment?

14. Recall the angel's promise to Mary: "The Lord God will give him the throne of his father David; . . . the child you bring to birth will be called Holy, Son of God" (Luke 1:33-35). Consider Mary's perspective here. What would be the hardest part of having to become less of a mother and more of a disciple?

A NOTE FROM EUGENE

TO BE A disciple, you have to think ahead. A good impulse isn't enough. Enthusiasm isn't enough. Good will isn't enough. Good intentions aren't enough. Discipleship involves deciding whether you want to get involved in a lifelong commitment. It is finding the resources you need to live obediently and act redemptively.

my brother and sister and mother."

FROM MARK 3, MSG

15. *How might Mary's song about God—"His mercy flows in wave after wave on those who are in awe before him" (Luke 1:50)—encourage her as she makes this transition from mother to disciple?*

16. *What do you find most challenging about "obeying God's will"? How does Mary's experience encourage you?*

Until we meet again

JESUS SEEMS *in this story to have revoked Mary's special privileges as his mother. Yet that's what we know her for today; as she sang in Luke 1, "What God has done for me will never be forgotten." Reflect on a time when you seemed to have lost some stature or prestige. How did God reassure you of his love for you?*

WHEN ARE YOU *tempted to treat Jesus as the crowds did—a kind of vending machine for miracles? Or as the religion scholars did—as a problematic theory of God to be resisted? Or as Jesus' family did—as someone who may think too highly of himself, or who owes you special treatment? Ask God this week to help you see Jesus for who he really is.*

Prayer

God, you are very kind to us. But not because of who we are. You are kind to us because you are kind.

You are also God. We recognize this as true; we also recognize that we sometimes behave as if you were something other than the Lord of the universe, the God who created us out of nothing.

Thank you that we can rely on your kindness—and that we don't have to rely on our own specialness for you to work for our good.

Mary

The Eyewitness to These Things

JOHN 19:23-35

WE ARE PARTICIPANTS and witnesses to life, but we are surrounded and threatened by death. The land of the living is like a war zone. And that's where we are stationed, to affirm the primacy of life over death, to give a witness to the connectedness and preciousness of all life, to engage in the practice of resurrection.

—EUGENE

1. *Recall a friend or loved one who has died. What did you most appreciate about them?*

2. *How did you grieve this lost loved one? What helped you celebrate life in the midst of your grief?*

WHEN THEY CRUCIFIED him, the Roman soldiers took his clothes and divided them up four ways, to each soldier a fourth. But his robe was seamless, a single piece of weaving, so they said to each other, "Let's not tear it up. Let's throw dice to see who gets it." This confirmed the Scripture that said, "They divided up my clothes among them and threw dice for my coat." (The soldiers validated the Scriptures!)

JOHN 19:23-24

3. *We're reminded in this passage that Jesus, Mary, and all the Jews were under the political authority of the Roman Empire. Why is Jesus' powerlessness here striking?*

4. *Even as the soldiers were demonstrating their power over Jesus and all the Jews, they unwittingly confirmed and "validated the Scriptures!" The prophecy referenced here is from Psalm 22:16-18: "Thugs gang up on me. They pin me down hand and foot. . . . They take my wallet and the shirt off my back, and then throw dice for my clothes." How does it make you feel to see that God spoke of such a sad and painful moment in Christian history long before it happened? Why?*

———————— ✁ ————————

WHILE THE SOLDIERS were looking after themselves, Jesus' mother, his aunt, Mary the wife of Clopas, and Mary Magdalene stood at the foot of the cross. Jesus saw his mother and the disciple he loved standing near her. He said to his mother, "Woman, here is your son." Then to the disciple, "Here is your mother." From that moment the disciple accepted her as his own mother.

JOHN 19:24-27 ——————————————————

5. The soldiers "were looking after themselves."
   Why do you think these soldiers are so casual
   and cavalier about an agonizing death?

6. While the soldiers looked after themselves, Mary and
   other family and friends of Jesus "stood at the foot
   of the cross." They couldn't prevent Jesus' death, so
   instead they witnessed it. What message would that
   send to the soldiers and others at the Crucifixion?

   What message would it send to Jesus?

A NOTE FROM EUGENE

NOTHING CAN PROVIDE more meaning to suffering than taking the suffering seriously, offering our companionship, and waiting in the dark with that person for the coming of dawn.

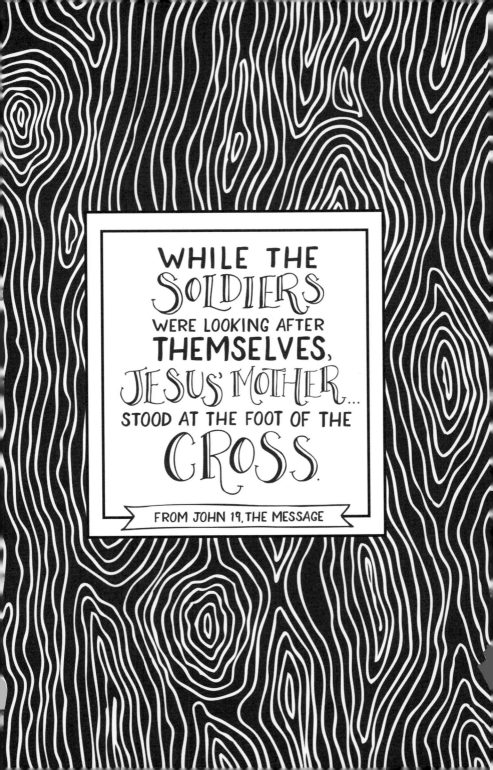

How can you serve as a witness in someone's hard situation right now?

7. Jesus sees his mother and his disciple from the cross. Why do you think he makes this connection between them? Why is this a priority for him during a time of such intense suffering?

8. The apostle Paul wrote that "anyone who neglects to care for family members in need repudiates the faith. That's worse than refusing to believe in the first place" (1 Timothy 5:8). How is Jesus caring for family members here?

What do you think will be involved in the disciple now treating Mary "as his own mother"?

*J*ESUS, SEEING THAT everything had been completed so that the Scripture record might also be complete, then said, "I'm thirsty."

A jug of sour wine was standing by. Someone put a sponge soaked with the wine on a javelin and lifted it to his mouth. After he took the wine, Jesus said, "It's done . . . complete." Bowing his head, he offered up his spirit.

Then the Jews, since it was the day of Sabbath preparation, and so the bodies wouldn't stay on the crosses over the Sabbath (it was a high holy day that year), petitioned Pilate that their legs be broken to speed death, and the bodies taken down. So the soldiers came and broke the legs of the first man crucified with Jesus, and then the other. When they got to Jesus, they saw that he was already dead, so they didn't break his legs. One of the soldiers stabbed him in the side with his spear. Blood and water gushed out.

JOHN 19:28-34

9. Jesus said, "I'm thirsty" so that "the Scripture record might also be complete." It was also in fulfillment of the Scriptures that the soldiers declined to break Jesus' bones. Why is it so important that Jesus' crucifixion "validated the Scriptures"?

10. Once "it [was] done . . . complete," Jesus "offered up his spirit" and died. Pause for a moment: What is significant about a God who dies? About a God who dies at the hands of people like us?

11. This isn't just the Son of God who dies; it's the son of Mary. If you were Mary, what would you be thinking and feeling at this moment?

*T*HE EYEWITNESS TO these things has presented an accurate report. He saw it himself and is telling the truth so that you, also, will believe.

JOHN 19:35

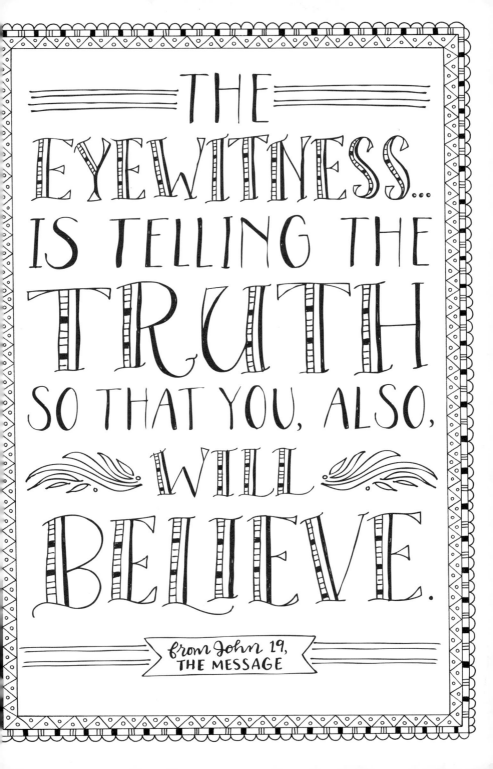

12. The eyewitness goes to great trouble to provide "*an accurate report . . . so that you, also, will believe.*" How could such a detailed account of Jesus' death help people believe in God?

    How does the Scripture account of Jesus' death impact your faith?

13. This passage ends with Jesus' death, but we know that three days later he is resurrected (see John 20). What does the resurrection of Jesus tell us about the death of Jesus? About the life of Jesus?

14. In this and most stories of Jesus' life, Mary, his mother, has a modest, quiet role. How does this reflect Mary's response to the angel: "*I'm the Lord's maid, ready to serve. Let it be with me just as you say*" (Luke 1:38)?

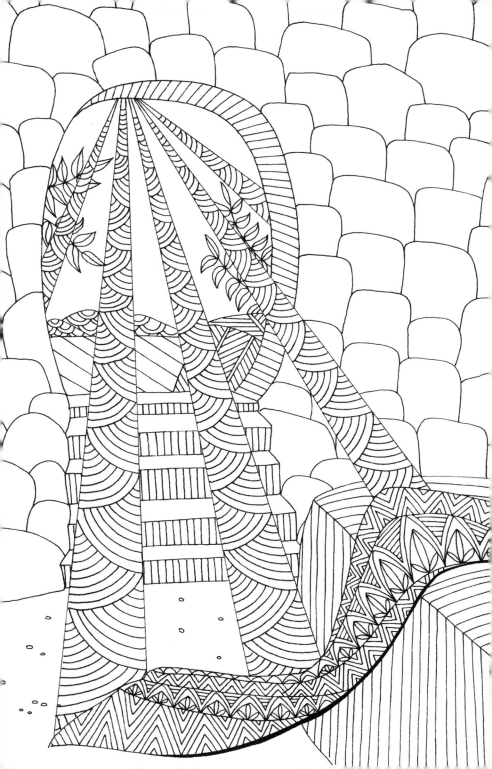

15. *What modest, quiet ways has God used you?*

*What would help you be prepared to say to God,
"I'm ready to serve. Let it be with me just as you say"?*

Until we meet again

CONSIDER *the people around you—your family, your neighbors, your coworkers. Who might Jesus want you to take care of on his behalf, the way his disciple took care of his mother on his behalf? Take some steps to actively care for that person this week.*

WHO DO YOU KNOW *who is suffering or grieving right now? Offer your companionship to them; wait in the dark with them for the light of dawn.*

AS WE'VE SEEN *throughout this study, Mary's relationship with Jesus operated on multiple levels: He was her son, but he was also her Lord. He looked after her and responded to her needs, but he didn't let her disrupt his divine mission. Mary, it turns out, is a model disciple in part due to this special relationship. Consider how you might lean into the loving, familiar relationship with Christ available to you; consider also what Jesus' lordship requires of you. How can you honor both aspects of this relationship?*

Prayer

God, you have filled me to overflowing with good news.
My relationship with you is a dance—I take joy in your love;
I submit to your leadership over my life.

Thank you for taking notice of me, for inviting me into your loving leadership.

Thank you for the strength you showed in your life and in your death.

Thank you for the mercy you show to me and others who need your love.

Thank you for the promise you make of a world based on your love and your truth.

Help me to orient my life around your love, your truth, to give a witness to the connectedness and preciousness of all life, to engage in the practice of resurrection.

The Scriptures not only reveal EVERYTHING of who God is BUT ALSO EVERYTHING of who we are.

Eugene Peterson

HOW TO LEAD A

Drawn in

BIBLE STUDY

⟋⟍⟋⟍

THE DOMINANT AND OBVIOUS FORMS of Christian discourse are preaching and teaching. That is as it should be. We have a great event of salvation to announce to the world. And we have a revealed truth about God and ourselves that we need to make as plain as possible. But there are other ways of using words that are just as important, if not as conspicuous: questions and conversations, comments and ruminations, counsel and suggestion. It's a quieter use of language and mostly takes place in times and locations that aren't set apart for religious discourse. It's the quieter conversational give-and-take of relationships in which we take each other seriously, respectfully attentive to what is said to us and thoughtfully responsive in what we say in return.

Our conversations with each other are sacred. Those that take place in the parking lot after Sunday worship are as much a part of the formation of Christian character as the preaching. But conversation, as such, is much neglected today as a form of Christian discourse. If we're to be in touch with all the parts of our lives and all the dimensions of the gospel, conversation requires equal billing (although not equal authority) with preaching and teaching.

The *Drawn in* Bible Studies can be a wonderful resource for personal Bible study. But because conversation is so valuable to our spiritual growth, consider working through the *Drawn in* Bible Studies with a group. Doing these studies together can be a wonderful way of enriching each person's understanding of the Scriptures, as well as an opportunity to grow deeper in relationship. Any number of benefits come from studying the Bible together, for example:

- New insights into God's Word
- Mutual encouragement
- Prayer for one another
- More robust relationships

These Bible studies are particularly good "on-ramps" for people who are new to the Bible, the practice of group or individual Bible study, or even the Christian faith. Non-Christians and new believers can be great participants in these studies, both for their own spiritual growth and for their fresh perspectives on what can be, for seasoned Bible study participants, overly familiar territory.

These Bible studies will also be rewarding for people of

all levels of spiritual maturity, offering a more reflective, creative approach to the small-group context.

As a leader, you will set the tone and manage the expectations of all participants. Not only the material you discuss but the environment you create for your group will send a message about who God is and how he relates to people. So give thought to how your meeting space can be warm and welcoming, how it can communicate compassion and care.

Because some questions invite vulnerability, and because people can be insecure about expressing their creative side, you'll want to establish and regularly reinforce the idea of grace and compassion as foundational to your group. Consider developing a "Bible study covenant" that each participant commits to, emphasizing these virtues. You'll also want to model vulnerability in how you engage the questions as they come up.

Your main job is to facilitate conversation. The study guide is a resource to that end. The questions are designed to be read out loud. Feel free to skip or rephrase a question if it seems out of sync with the overall discussion. If your group discussion is particularly robust, feel the freedom to select only a few key questions from each chapter. Be sure to allow time and space for group members to raise their own questions about the passage you're studying.

You'll also want to manage people's expectations. Be sure to clearly establish start and finish times with as much consistency as possible. Have coloring tools on hand if people want to continue to doodle as you discuss the passage.

Your job isn't to teach, and you don't have to have a ready answer for every question that comes up. It's okay to say, "I don't know" or "Does anyone have thoughts on that question?" Still, it's good to come prepared. As you review the session before your meeting, give some thought to the people in your group—what in the passage is likely to trip them up or cause them confusion? Which questions might touch on tender spots for them? How can you be a good support for your group members as the group is meeting?

Most of all, enjoy this time with one another. You are not alone in the leadership of this group; the Holy Spirit will be moving within you and your group members. Allow yourself grace as you lead, and look for opportunities to step aside and witness the Spirit at work.

May the creativity and reflection that this guide fosters lead to good discussion and rich friendships for you and your group!

NOTES FOR SESSION ONE

Some participants may have trouble situating Mary (see question 2). A quick overview of the time and place—first-century Palestine, ruled over by the Roman Empire, in a regional town (Nazareth) often dismissed by the more cosmopolitan Jerusalem (see, for example, John 1:45-46). The point is that Jesus was born to modest circumstances, far from the halls of power. Certainly Mary would not have anticipated a direct role for herself in the world-shaping events of Jesus' life, death, and resurrection.

Some participants may not be able to relate to a discussion of "an encounter with God" (question 4). If you know of some group members who are good at articulating their experience of a relationship with God, this might be a good place to invite them to share.

Are Mary's life prospects really "not great" (question 5)? In addition to the general circumstances Mary finds herself in (see question 2), be prepared to discuss first-century cultural attitudes toward women (for example, they were not considered credible witnesses in court; divorce and property laws were prejudiced against them). Whereas a woman found pregnant without being married today might suffer some isolated shame and rejection, in first-century Palestine this would be scandalous.

Some members of your group may have "miracle stories" to affirm the angel's assertion that "nothing . . . is impossible with God" (see question 8). If you know of someone in your group with such a story, you may want to invite them to share it. But be careful: On the one hand, some group members might want to call something that happened to them "miraculous" simply to draw attention to themselves; meanwhile, other group members may be especially suspicious of the miraculous, or may be discouraged that they don't have such a story to share.

The promises Mary sings about (see question 15) are

not simply about her specifically; as a devout Jew, Mary identifies herself with the covenant promises God made to Israel, "beginning with Abraham" (the assurance that he would become a great nation through which other nations would be blessed—see Genesis 12:1-3) and continuing through Moses and the deliverance from Egyptian slavery; David's kingship and the promise from God that the Messiah would come from his line; and so on and so forth. Mary's very personal experience with the angel is simultaneously the fulfillment of a promise God made repeatedly to his people.

Be prepared to guide the group through the question "What promises has God made to you?" Consider biblical assurances—"I will be with you," "I have good plans for you," and so on. But don't preempt participation by group members; invite them to reflect on what promises they are counting on from God.

NOTES FOR SESSION TWO

Jesus' words to Mary, "This isn't my time" (question 5), can be confusing, especially to people who are relatively new to Christianity. Consider a brief discussion of chronological time versus *kairos*, or "opportune time." Jesus' sense of mission is in view here; he has come to earth to fulfill all God's promises to Israel and to deliver us from our sin, but there is much to be done first, and while Jesus is sovereign as God in the flesh, he also submits himself (including his time) to God the Father.

The notion that "Jesus could be talked into a miracle" (see question 7, part two) is somewhat provocative. Be prepared for this question to open up some discussion. At the heart of this question is a discussion of prayer: Why do we pray? Can we influence God by our prayers? Is God really sovereign if our prayers can change his plans? Ultimately the dynamics of prayer are a mystery—be sure to emphasize this in your discussion—but consider offering some biblical parameters for prayer: from testing our motives beforehand (see James 4:1-10) to emulating Jesus' prayer in the garden of Gethsemane, asserting your desire but yielding to God's will (Matthew 26:36-46). The psalmist concisely explains both the promise and the parameters of our prayer: "Keep company with GOD, get in on the best. Open up before GOD, keep nothing back; he'll do whatever needs to be done" (Psalm 37:3-6).

NOTES FOR SESSION THREE

The opening comment from Eugene and the first couple of questions in this session may be particularly tender. By this point in the study, some participants may be realizing that they've formed opinions about Jesus based on hearsay or negative experiences or any number of other influences. This direct study of the Bible may be threatening some of their perspectives on God. Others may be becoming disillusioned with the people who shaped their beliefs about God. Be gentle with your group. The positive message in these opening questions is that the Bible offers a unique perspective into the character of God, a perspective that eludes many well-intentioned people—people like Jesus' family, including his mother. Moreover, there are some people whose opinions about God are tainted by their own self-importance, their own need to be right, their own bad experiences. There is no bad outcome to testing our opinions about God, and the opinions of those we care about, against what we see directly of Jesus in the Bible. Some of those opinions may well be affirmed! But the Bible's portrait of God in Christ will always stretch us, always pleasantly surprise us.

"Devil tricks" (question 7) is obviously not a technical term, but it may prove confusing to some. Be prepared to prime the conversation with observations about spiritually abusive or exploitative behavior with a religious gloss. Financial misconduct, sexual scandal, televangelists—there are, sadly, many examples your group could consider.

Parents with rebellious children may find questions 11–13 a little tender. Jesus certainly seems dismissive, even derisive, toward his family here. Isn't there a commandment about honoring your parents? And yet the Bible assures us that Jesus was without sin (see Hebrews 4:15). So something else is happening here. Help your group wrestle with how Jesus' interaction with the crowd and his family in this passage might both honor his relationship as an adult child to his mother and fulfill his divinely ordained mission.

In many ways this passage from Mark 3 reflects the various ways we can relate to Jesus that miss the mark of God's intentions for us. The crowds related to Jesus as though he were a vending machine, "making demands on him." His friends were worried about him but "suspected he was getting carried away with himself"; they honored him to a point, but didn't want to acknowledge Jesus' lordship. The religion scholars saw him as a threat and treated him as such. And his family saw themselves as having special privileges with him; they were surprised when his mission took priority over their wishes. If even Mary had to learn to think differently about Jesus—as not just her son but her Lord—then we, too, will have to regularly test our attitudes when we approach him.

NOTES FOR SESSION FOUR

Death is always a tender subject—and not the most exciting topic to begin a group discussion! If you know of members of your group for whom recalling a loved one who has died will be particularly difficult, consider a softer start to this chapter than questions 1–2. Eugene reflects not just on death here but on life; invite group members "to give a witness to the connectedness and preciousness of all life." Draw the group's attention to recent signs of life in your midst—a wedding, a birth, a graduation, a new job, something that can be celebrated by all. Once you've acknowledged the preciousness of life, move gently into the topic of death.

Question 4 draws our attention to the prophecy about Jesus' crucifixion in Psalm 22. This is the psalm Jesus quotes from the cross: "My God, my God, why have you abandoned me?" (Mark 15:33-34; see also Psalm 22:1). The focus of this study is on Mary, but feel free to spend some time discussing Jesus' experience on the cross and its implications for us. Some group members may never have considered the price Jesus paid for their salvation; some may never have embraced Jesus as their Savior. Be attentive to the Spirit's work in your group during this discussion.

The demeanor of the soldiers (see question 5) is striking in our time; we don't expect to see people so cavalier about death, particularly violent death. And yet violence is a characteristic of our own time—in far-off war zones and under totalitarian regimes, and even close to home, in violence-charged cities and abuse-plagued families near us. If your group would benefit from the discussion, invite participants to reflect on where they see the attitude of the soldiers in contemporary life.

Questions 7–8 demonstrate a running theme about Jesus: He is kind, loving, attentive to our needs. Mary needs someone to look after her; so does "the disciple he loved." How often do we lose sight of the needs of others as we are suffering? But for Jesus, the needs of others remained in view; indeed, his crucifixion was an act willingly undertaken because of our need for deliverance from our sin.

The prophecies highlighted in question 9 are from Psalm 42:1-3 ("I'm thirsty for God-alive. I wonder, 'Will I ever make it—arrive and drink in God's presence?'") and Psalm 34:19-20, 22 ("GOD is there every time. He's your bodyguard, shielding every bone; not even a finger gets broken. . . . No one who runs to him loses out"). Similarly, Jesus' crucifixion evokes the lamb sacrificed at Passover: "Don't break any of the bones" (Exodus 12:46). Jesus' death is the fulfillment of the story of Scripture.

Question 13 alludes to the Resurrection, but that's just the beginning: Because of Jesus' sacrifice on our behalf, we are no longer enslaved by death. Our destiny becomes life forever with our Savior in the Kingdom of God. Remind your group that the Kingdom of God reflects the character of Christ—who, we've learned in this study, is full of grace and truth and loving-kindness.

DISCOVER THE DELIGHT OF BEING

Drawn in

From her simple faithfulness as a young woman to her soul-piercing anguish at the foot of the cross, journey with Mary through the sorrows and the joys of saying yes to God.

Ruth's resilience and resourcefulness offer you a creative vision for navigating life's inevitable struggles, trusting God, and holding fast to his irrevocable hope.

Esther's courage and conviction will help you discover how to find your voice and grow your faith during times of trouble.

Become the Woman
God Created You to Be